How to Craft an Effective Agenda

 *effective meetings*
S E R I E S

How to Craft an Effective Agenda

How to Chair an Effective Meeting

How to Take Minutes Effectively

How to
Craft an Effective Agenda

Debi J. Peverill

Copyright ©2022 Debi J. Peverill

Published by Painless Financial Training Group Inc
5 Florence Street,
Lower Sackville, Nova Scotia
Canada B4J 1C5

Reproduction of this material in whole or in part without written authorization, by any duplication process whatsoever, both present and future, is a violation of copyright and offenders risk prosecution.

Disclaimer: Nothing in this book is intended to replace advice which is specific to your circumstances. This book is for educational purposes and is not professional advice.

ISBN: 978-1-989228-14-2 (paperback)
ISBN: 978-1-989228-12-8 (e-book)

How to Craft an Effective Agenda

Contents

Chapter 1: Effective Agendas Make Effective Meetings 1
- *Meeting or Not* 2
- *About an Agenda* 5
- *To Do* 7

Chapter 2: Creating the Agenda 9
- *Standard Agenda Format* 9
- *Policy Reviews* 14
- *Responsibility for Creating the Agenda* 16
- *Timing of Each Agenda Item* 18
- *Order of the Agenda Items* 19
- *To Do* 21

Chapter 3: Meeting Attendees 23
- *Members* 23
- *Guests* 25
- *Uninviting People from Meetings* 27
- *To Do* 28

Chapter 4: Draft Agenda 29
- *Conflict of Interest* 30
- *Time for Consideration of Agenda Items* 31
- *Items on the Agenda to Be Removed* 31
- *To Do* 32

Chapter 5: Scheduling the Meeting 33
- *Standard Meeting Times* 33
- *Non-Standard Meeting Schedules* 34
- *Timing* 35
- *Quorum* 36
- *To Do* 37

Chapter 6: Virtual Meetings 39
- *Agendas* 39
- *Frequency* 40

Polling *40*
Meeting Credentials or Signing In *40*
To Do *41*

Chapter 7: Confidential Items and Conflicts of Interest 43
Confidential Items *43*
Privacy Officer *46*
Conflict of Interest. *46*
In Camera *47*
To Do *49*

Chapter 8: Annual General Meetings. 51
To Do *54*

Chapter 9: Receiving an Agenda – A Guide for Participants 55
Scheduling. *55*
Review the Agenda Promptly. *55*
Think about the Decisions *56*
To Do *58*

Glossary. 59

Appendix A: Policies to Consider 63
Meeting Administration *63*
Meeting Planning Policies *69*
During-the-Meeting Policies *74*
Virtual Meeting Policies *77*
Annual General Meeting Policies *80*

Appendix B: Consolidated List of Things to Do 81

Other Books by Debi J. Peverill 87

About the Author 89

For More Information. 91

1 Effective Agendas Make Effective Meetings

We all spend time in meetings—wouldn't it be great if all the meetings were effective?

What do I mean by an effective meeting?

> *An effective meeting achieves the goal of the meeting in a reasonable amount of time without undue drama or stress.*

Have you been at a meeting like this: You don't know the goal of the meeting, you don't know who is invited, and no one has given you an agenda? This is a meeting that is doomed to failure. The information in this book will help you avoid hosting or attending any more of these doomed meetings.

Crafting an effective agenda increases attendance at your meetings. More people will show up to a meeting when they are interested in the topics that will be discussed.

You might also expect a good turnout if the agenda includes any contentious issues.

The agenda can have the opposite effect as well. If a potential attendee looks at the agenda and does not see anything they are interested in discussing, they may not attend the meeting.

If you want to have effective meetings, then the first step is to learn how to prepare an effective agenda.

Meeting or Not

Is it possible you could handle what needs to be done with a phone call, a memo, a document, a spreadsheet, an email, or a walk in the park?

Many people hate meetings, and calling one should be a strategic choice, done only when all other options have been considered and discarded.

Of course, after you apply what you learn by reading this book, your meetings are going to be very effective, and people will not object to being invited to one of yours. I promise.

Meetings do serve a purpose. Meetings will never be gone from our lives. Here are some situations where a meeting is necessary:

* More than one person needs to make a decision.

- ✸ Material needs to be presented and discussed, not just read.
- ✸ The group needs to keep its identity. Getting together at a meeting is a part of what defines the team. The board meeting is for the board, the marketing meeting is for the marketing committee.

Decisions Need to Be Made

Board meetings are a prime example of a necessary meeting.

The board makes decisions, and it needs to have the input of all board members before the decision can be made. Also, the meeting defines the board – only board members may attend the meeting and only members can vote on the decisions. Being at the board meeting defines who the board is and what the board is doing.

Board decisions are made by voting and recording the result of the vote. This is much easier in person or virtually. It does not work well as a series of emails, but it can be done, if necessary. The board meeting is probably the clearest example of a situation where only a meeting will achieve the goal.

Material Needs to Be Understood

Meetings are sometimes necessary to teach people new skills.

People absorb information in different ways. Some

people prefer to read on their own – give them the manual, and they will figure it out. Others are visual or auditory learners, and they will benefit from being with others to understand new procedures. The tactile learners have to physically do something in order to understand.

If your group is going to be successful in teaching people new skills, it will need to create opportunities for people to hear from an instructor, ask questions, and perform exercises.

If you send out learning material without any other type of follow-up, some people will not understand this material. Sending out the material and then having a meeting of some description will be more effective. This is a valid reason for holding a meeting.

Group Identity Needs to Be Created or Maintained

Team building is an important activity for most groups. The weekly check-in is standard for many organizations. Sure, you could replace the check-in with a document that lists everyone's meetings and goals for the week. That document is a good thing to have as well. But the meeting is useful for humans to feel connected to their team.

Virtual meetings can serve this purpose, but there is more information available to us when we meet in person. We see more of the other people at the meeting not just their heads or their name floating in a black box.

There is also more casual chat at an in-person meeting. People are social animals, and some meetings are necessary if you are building a team.

Now that you have decided to hold a meeting, we move on to crafting the agenda.

About an Agenda

An agenda is the list of the topics that will be discussed at the meeting in the order in which they will be dealt with.

This book is all about agendas, the starting point of an effective meeting. The book includes a list of all the meeting policies that affect the agenda and the steps a participant should take in preparing for the meeting.

The agenda is the planning for the meeting and – if you spend a little time planning, you get better results.

I have written other books about meetings. If you are interested in how to chair a meeting or how to take minutes, check out the other books in this series.

You don't have to read the whole book all at once, although it is not long. You can read the chapter titles and decide which chapters would be the most useful to you.

Purpose

Potential participants need to be informed about what will be discussed. Many people will not attend a meeting unless they are given an agenda. Unless the boss tells them, they have to attend!

It is also important to let people know whether they will be making a decision at the meeting or providing input for someone else to make a decision. If they are providing input, they need to know what preparation they should undertake.

Strategic Plan

The strategic plan is key to an organization achieving its goals, and the agenda is the plan on how the goals will be achieved at each meeting.

The strategic plan will have been divided up into goals and objectives. Each of these goals has a time line and a metric for when it will be achieved. These metrics should be assigned to the various board meetings that will take place during the time frame of the strategic plan.

Having the goals of the organization on the agenda is a reminder of why there is a meeting, what is going to be accomplished at the meeting, and how the meeting fits into the overall strategy of the organization.

The agenda is not a silo; it is a part of the system that will lead to effective meetings, and effective meetings will help the organization achieve their goals.

To Do

Look at the meeting schedule in your organization.

- ✓ Analyze whether each meeting is necessary or if there might be another way to achieve the goal.
- ✓ See if you can eliminate 10 percent of the meetings on your schedule and replace them with shared documents or an email thread.
- ✓ Determine what the goal is for each of these meetings you deem necessary.

Creating the Agenda

An effective meeting includes some common agenda items.

Standard Agenda Format

1. Call to order
2. Motion to Approve the Agenda
3. Motion to Approve the Prior Meeting's Minutes
4. Financial Statements
5. Reports and Decision Items (may include any of the following)
    i. Reports from Standing Committees
    ii. Reports from Ad Hoc Committees
    iii. Officers' Reports
    iv. Actions from the Strategic Plan
    v. Action Items

6. Meeting Evaluation
7. Adjournment

This is the bare bones of what should be on an agenda. Obviously, each group will make their own decisions about what else to include.

Reports from Standing Committees

If your group has committees, each committee will make a report at each meeting. A standing committee is a committee that always exists; it fulfills an ongoing function such as a fundraising committee or nominating committee. It is possible the committee report will be included in the board package and the committee chair can merely say, "You have my report, does anyone have any questions?"

The committee might want to emphasize some item of their progress or ask for help or feedback from the group. There is no point in reading a report at a meeting. Your policies should prohibit this.

Your organization could choose to use a consent agenda. In this case, reports that don't need a discussion or a motion can be accepted as presented in a single motion. Board members should be reminded that they still have to read the reports, and any questions they have must be raised at the meeting.

Reports from Ad Hoc Committees

The opposite of a standing committee is the ad hoc committee. An ad hoc committee is more topical; there is a current issue that needs to be addressed. This committee may need more time to bring items to the board for discussion. They will disband when they have achieved the goal of the committee.

Officers Reports

Officers may also have a report. The president may want to comment on any activities since the last meeting. The secretary may have some correspondence they would like to explain.

It is possible the officers will write up their reports, and then take questions or hit the highlights of the report for the group.

Strategic Plan

Not every group has a strategic plan. But any standing committee, working group, or board of directors will benefit from the strategic planning exercise. If your meetings are less formal, you need a meeting goal instead of a strategic plan. Any actions from either the strategic plan or the meeting goals need to be on the agenda.

Action Items

Some groups include a list of action items at the end of the agenda so participants can keep track of what they agreed to do. Participants will look at the minutes for the list of action items, in general, but some groups want to see the action items on the agenda.

Meeting Evaluation

The second-last item on the agenda should be determining whether the goals of the meeting were achieved and listening to any feedback to improve future meetings. This standard agenda item is a best practice for having effective meetings.

First, how do you measure the effectiveness of the meeting? Is there a difference between the effectiveness of the meeting and the effectiveness of the person who chairs the meeting?

Let's start with easy stuff:

- Was the agenda circulated ahead of the meeting?
- Did the meeting have quorum?
- Did the meeting start on time?
- Was everyone able to reach agreement on the decisions?
- Were all the items on the agenda dealt with?
- Did the meeting end on time?

The above questions can be answered with a yes or no, and the participants will probably agree on most of these answers.

More challenging questions . . .

- Did you participate?
- Did you feel comfortable expressing your viewpoint?
- Did the meeting accomplish the stated goals?

You can ask the questions in various ways. For the easy ones, you can track these metrics without much difficulty by asking for a show of hands. For example, you can ask, "Did you receive your agenda ahead of the meeting?" the participants will raise their hands, the chair can count the hands, and a determination made. This might be a time for a quick discussion if there are any participants who did not get the agenda.

The first six questions could be asked and answered in this way. The other questions are more delicate, and less confident participants might not speak up. This part might best be done with a paper evaluation to be handed in or an emailed form.

If the feedback needs to be anonymous and the meeting is virtual, then a survey could be sent – or the polling function in the virtual meeting software, could be used and set up to be anonymous.

Using polling to do the meeting evaluation will be quicker than verbally asking the questions, but the polling must be set up and someone must do that.

During the meeting, the results of the polls will need to be recorded by the person who is taking the minutes.

Adjournment

The very last thing that happens at the meeting is the motion to adjourn. Your group will have a policy about which rules of order they are following. If you are using *Robert's*, the motion to adjourn does not require a seconder, only a majority in favour. If you are using *Bourinot's*, then you only require a seconder, and there is no debate on the motion.

Policy Reviews

Every organization has policies. Policies need constant review and development to be effective. How should you handle this on your agenda?

One Policy Meeting a Year

Some groups like to do all their policy work at one big meeting held annually. I imagine some people would love to miss the meeting at which the policies are going to be discussed.

If you are going to have a policy review meeting, then the agenda will be divided up into sections and there will probably not be much else on that meeting's agenda. You should consider frequent breaks, lots of caffeine, and a punishment for anyone who is going to be absent.

Every Agenda

If policy review is always on the agenda, participants will not be able to escape participating in the review.

If you make policy reviews a standard agenda item, the board can deal with one or two at a time and do a better job of it.

Three-Year Cycle

Best practices suggest you review all your policies every three years. If you were to take the policies you have and divide by the number of meetings you have in a three-year time period, you know how many policies you have to review each meeting.

Procedure for Policy Review

Circulate the policy to be reviewed with the board package, unless your policies are all on a website, then let the participants know which policies are going to be reviewed at the meeting.

What does policy review mean? The process could be as simple as reading the policy and deciding whether there are any changes that need to be made. Has anything happened that means this policy is no longer needed? You could ask subject matter experts if they have any suggestions for changes and bring that feedback to the meeting.

Some policies are going to require more attention than

others, and sometimes you need to create a policy where you did not have one before.

Policy Committee

Maybe you have a policy committee. This group would meet frequently and stick to the time table of reviewing all the policies within a three-year time period. If this is your situation, you create a standing agenda item for the committee who reports to the board. The board would then ratify the committee's recommendations.

Responsibility for Creating the Agenda

Board Meetings

Board meetings are a formal affair. The board has a strategic plan, roles and responsibilities, and terms of reference. It is the chair's responsibility to initially establish the items on the agenda, and then the agenda is circulated for approval, additions, and deletions by the members of the group.

For a board meeting, the first step when creating an agenda is to consult the strategic plan. Each meeting has a role to play in implementing the strategic plan. The tasks on the strategic plan should be divided up between all the meetings to be held that year.

After the tasks from the strategic plan are on the agenda, what else should be added?

The agenda is formally approved at the actual meeting.

Non-Board Meetings

If your group is not a board, the group itself will decide who creates and controls the agenda. What should that decision involve? The following questions should be answered by your group.

- Who can add items to the agenda?
- Who decides how long the agenda will be?
- Who decides in what order the agenda items should be dealt with?

Meeting Organizer Sets the Agenda

Sometimes, the person who calls the meeting sets the agenda. This is more likely to be the case if the meeting is not a formal board meeting, an Annual General Meeting (AGM), or a committee meeting.

Suppose a co-worker says, "We need to get together to look at the sales budget for the third quarter and make a recommendation to the executive team." That is an agenda, you know what the goal is, you know what you need to do, and you probably know who is invited. This informal meeting has a clear agenda and a clear outcome.

The next step is to determine what material needs to be prepared ahead of the meeting and reviewed by the participants so that the meeting itself will be efficient.

Boss

What about when the boss gives a group an agenda item. You don't tell the boss that she can't tell you what to do, since a large part of the role of a boss is the actual bossing around. However, it is helpful if the group has a terms-of-reference document so that it is clear what topics will be discussed at a meeting.

As a part of the terms of reference for the group, decide who is going to control the agenda and document it. Then all the stakeholders know whether they are allowed to add items to the agenda or not and who has the final say on whether an item is on the agenda or not.

As a part of the terms of reference, the group should have a list of topics for which they are responsible. These are the topics that belong on an agenda.

Timing of Each Agenda Item

How long will each item on the agenda take to deal with? An estimate can be made, but predicting the future is not a common skill, so some allowances will need to be made.

If you tell participants how long to expect each item to be discussed, it does give them an idea of how important the issue is to the organization. Some groups will put the time on the agenda. If the meeting starts at 9 am, the time to approve the agenda might be at 9.05 and the prior minutes at 9.10, and so forth.

I am an auditor and when I am invited to attend a board meeting or an AGM, I sometimes see that they have allocated five minutes for a discussion of the audited financial statements. This tells me the importance they attach to their audited financial statements!

There may be arguments about how long the group should spend on any issue. Whenever you have a number of people together, they may disagree about the relevance of topics. There will be some negotiation needed in the drafting of the agenda. However, if this can be done before the actual meeting, the meeting itself will proceed more efficiently.

Order of the Agenda Items

How important is it, to have the agenda in a logical order?

The call to order has to be first. The approval of the agenda is typically the next item up. After that, the other items can be ordered in various ways.

Group Similar Items

It is logical to put all the financial stuff together: review of the receivables list, financial statements, and the comparison to budget. The entire finance or audit committee report could be handled all at one time. Then you might put all the employee reports together. It should save time to talk about similar items at the same time.

Even the board members with the shortest attention spans should be able to get through a section of content without having some concept explained again. If you split up the financial stuff, a board member might forget what they understand about financial information between the beginning and the end of the meeting.

Contentious Issues

Do you put the contentious items first or last or sandwich them in the middle? Do you want to get the board agreeing on a few items before you introduce any items on which the board is unlikely to agree. Or maybe you want to get the contentious stuff over with so that by the time the meeting ends the disagreement was hours ago.

Is there a risk that a board member will become so agitated when discussing the contentious issue that they will not be willing to continue to participate? Any chance someone is going to storm out of the meeting or resign? If so, do you want to get that over with or wait until the end of the meeting?

Pacing and Tempo

Can you alternate the dry portions of the meeting with more interesting items? Meetings with a lot of items on the agenda need some variety to keep the participants from nodding off.

Is there a benefit to keeping an important or popular agenda item until the end of the meeting? The participants may be tired by then, or they may be waiting for this one item to be discussed.

Do you want to have the best part of the meeting at the end of the meeting so the participants will stay until the end?

To Do

- ✓ Develop a generic agenda on which to base each individual meeting's agenda. Include the minimum agenda items and add any items unique to the organization.

- ✓ Decide whether to use a consent agenda for those reports that don't need discussion.

- ✓ Decide whether you will have any actions from the strategic plan (if you have one) on your agenda.

- ✓ Decide whether your agenda should include meeting evaluation as the second-last item on the agenda. Decide what questions you want to ask and how you are going to ask them. Set up the polls for votes ahead of time.

- ✓ Decide how your organization deals with policy review: Do you need to schedule an annual or quarterly policy review meeting? Or is there a committee? Or maybe you should put the policy review on each meeting agenda?

- ✓ For every standard meeting, set a policy about the development of the agenda and document the process. Document who is allowed to add items to the agenda, how the agenda is circulated, how it is approved, how differences of opinion concerning the agenda will be dealt with, and so forth.

- ✓ The duration for the meeting should also be established, and you may want to assign a time to each agenda item.

3 Meeting Attendees

Deciding who to invite is an important part of the preparation for the meeting and the drafting of the agenda. You could have members, observers, or guests. Or maybe the meeting is open to anyone. If guests are coming, they need to know when they should show up. Put that information on the agenda.

Depending on the type of meeting, there might be a restriction on who can attend. Who should have a role to play in the meeting should be based on the goals of the organization or the meeting.

Members

Do you need to be a member to attend the meeting? For example, if this is a committee meeting, only committee members are invited to the meeting, and all of them must be invited. You can't call it a committee meeting if you do not invite all the members.

If there is no membership, it will take more thought to decide who to invite to the meeting. Back to the goal, what are you trying to accomplish at this meeting? If this is a training meeting, you should invite everyone who needs the training. If that is too many people, multiple meetings with the same agenda should be scheduled.

If the goal of the meeting is to make decisions, consider who needs to be at the meeting to achieve the goal? Is there an ideal number of people at the meeting? Too many and the meeting takes forever, too few and you probably can't decide anything because you are missing expertise and experience you need.

Ex-Officio Members

Ex-officio means members who are literally appointed to the group because of their position. For example, the president of a provincial or state group might automatically be a part of the federal group. Ex-officio attendees are generally full members of the group, entitled to a vote on all matters. Ex-officio board members are appointed, and other board members are elected by the members.

An ex-officio member is appointed by another group, not your group. Your group has no control over who fills this position in your group. The position is on your board, but the occupant is appointed elsewhere.

Some groups have reciprocal memberships. For example, the president of the local tourism organization may be invited to be on the board of the local board of trade and vice versa.

Set a time limit for re-evaluating when some office is needed on the board and when they are not.

Guests

You can invite guests to any meeting. A guest can be invited to the entire meeting or to only a portion of the meeting. The guests, of course, do not have a vote at the meeting. You can also determine how much the guest can contribute. Are they there to talk or listen?

A guest could be there for a couple of reasons. Sometimes the guest is a subject matter expert (SME), a committee chair, or an observer.

A guest could also be thinking about joining the board. They want to see how the board operates before they make a commitment to the group. If this is the case, the participants should be on their best behaviour because board members are hard to find!

The group's auditor will be invited to the meeting when the board reviews the financial statements. Sometimes this is done by an audit committee or a finance committee. Either way, the auditor will be a guest at the meeting.

Subject Matter Experts (SMEs)

In some cases, you want to ask a guest to come in – possibly a subject matter expert who can give a presentation to help the participants understand a technical issue and to provide advice. If the subject matter expert is meeting with the group, it is because there is a need for discussion and questions and answers. Otherwise, the SME could provide a written report, and the members could read it at their leisure.

This guest can come in at a specific time and leave when their time on the agenda is over.

Committee Chairs

A committee chair might attend a board meeting to explain and report on the activities of that particular committee. The committee member does not have a vote at the board meeting. They arrive at an appointed time, make their report, and then leave.

Observers

Observers are sometimes invited, or they sometimes invite themselves. An observer does just that – they do not contribute, and they do not have a vote. In fact, some organizations make it very clear an observer should not be talking or interacting in any way with the rest of the participants.

Funders sometimes ask to attend as observers. A funder

might require invitations to meetings as a requirement for the organization to receive the funding. They have provided money and they want to be sure the money is being spent in accordance with the terms of the agreement. In some groups, the observer will not even answer direct questions; they take the observer part very seriously.

However, the very presence of observers can dampen the discussion at a meeting. There is a sense that the group is being judged. Perhaps an observer is only welcome during the portion of the meeting where the relevant decisions are being made. Again, this will be noted on the agenda.

Uninviting People from Meetings

Are there participants you would like to uninvite? If you have a person who is not helping the cause, the group could decide to vote them off the island. Policies and terms of reference may apply.

What provisions do you have for removing people who are not helping with achieving the goal? Is it possible to remove participants who are not behaving well? The group should have some rules about how to behave.

To Do

✓ Decide who is and is not invited to the meeting: ex-officio members, SMEs, committee chairs, observers. Set a time limit for re-evaluating when some ex officio office is needed on the board and when they are not.

✓ Determine whether you have a way to change who is invited or to uninvite someone who has been attending the meeting, either for their behaviour or because they are not contributing.

4 Draft Agenda

THE AGENDA SHOULD be circulated to potential participants at least a week before the meeting. Participants need time to do the following:

- review the topics and potentially add items to the agenda
- read any reports that will be presented
- determine whether they have a conflict of interest with any of the items to be discussed
- decide whether they are going to attend and let the chair know

Details of circulating an agenda containing confidential items are discussed in chapter 7.

After the agenda is sent out, the board package that contains all the background material needs to be circulated.

Sometimes the board package will need to be changed based on the circulation of the agenda.

Conflict of Interest

A conflict of interest arises when a board member is asked to make a decision that could lead to them receiving a personal benefit. Upon starting on a board, the board member has agreed to keep the best interests of the organization in mind. Therefore, a board member will need to recuse themselves from the part of the meeting when the conflicted item will be discussed.

Conflict of interest is one reason for the agenda to be circulated prior to the board package. For each participant who declares a conflict of interest, the board package must be modified to prevent this participant from seeing the information where they have a conflict.

The agenda is an important part of the conflict-of-interest policy. Participants must identify and declare their conflicts at this point in the process, before they have seen the information they should not see. Once they have looked at the information, it is too late to discover the conflict. You cannot unring that bell. See chapter 7 for more details about how to handle conflict of interest.

Time for Consideration of Agenda Items

Allowing all the participants to prepare for the meeting means the participants have had a chance to consider the items on the agenda and get additional information if needed. Participants can make better decisions when they have had more time to think about the issues.

When you put items on the agenda at the last minute, participants may not have a chance to consider the issue carefully enough. Sometimes people do this on purpose.

Reflecting on an issue can often uncover problems that need to be addressed. Few things are as simple as they initially appear, so taking a little time to make a decision is generally wise.

Items on the Agenda to Be Removed

Sometimes a participant will believe an item on the agenda is not board business. They might feel that a committee should deal with the item first or that the board should not deal with the item at all.

A board is responsible for setting the strategic direction of the organization and management is responsible for implementation. A board member might think there are items on the agenda that are matters of implementation or operational issues, and thus should not be addressed by the board at all.

Board members should be clear on their role and able to decide what items belong on the agenda and what items do not. Sometimes a board will see some creep in their role. This is referred to as mission creep or scope creep, and it is a dangerous issue. If the board is seeing role creep, they might start thinking more items require their attention and the meetings get longer and less focused.

To Do

- ✓ Establish a policy about circulating the agenda. This policy should include how it is circulated, who gets it, how long before the meeting it is circulated, and the methods and deadlines to be used to add items to the agenda or to ask for items to be removed.

5 Scheduling the Meeting

The scheduling of the meeting is a very important task. Some groups will have a standing meeting time, while others meet irregularly.

Who is responsible for scheduling the meetings and for figuring out if there is going to be a quorum for an upcoming meeting? Keeping track of attendance and reminding people about the meeting can take up a bunch of time. Who should be doing that?

Does the chair have staff? Does the group have staff? This is a staff function.

Standard Meeting Times

A standard meeting time means that the group or board meets at the same time each week or month, such as the second Tuesday of each month. This makes it easier for people to remember to attend and to get it into their schedule as a recurring event.

A standard meeting time, however, means that some participants will never be able to attend because they have a conflict with a Tuesday meeting. There have been some fascinating conversations at meetings I have attended about the benefits of either a Tuesday or a Wednesday standard meeting date. I wish I could get that time back.

There is a benefit to the standard meeting time, and your group might consider adopting this policy.

Non-Standard Meeting Schedules

Some groups are not going to meet every month. They may meet irregularly or meet every quarter or every second week.

Groups have had some success with picking the date of the next meeting at the end of the current meeting. This works as long as the group is not too large. A group of fifteen people making a decision about the next meeting two months away is going to take a long time to decide on a date, and still someone is not going to be happy about that.

There is an app for that. You can set up a software app that allows everyone to enter times they are available, and the software does the calculations from there. Much time is saved and you can blame the software for the choice, which might be less contentious.

Look at the amount of time spent talking about scheduling the next meeting and think about whether a standard meeting date would save time.

Sending Regrets

No matter how the group schedules its meetings, participants are encouraged to let the organizers know in plenty of time that they are not going to be able to attend the meeting. Most meetings require a quorum. People will get annoyed if there is no quorum when they show up for a meeting.

Participants need to understand they are expected to attend. Only important events should keep them from a scheduled meeting. Walking the dog or washing your hair, while important to you, are not good reasons for not attending the meeting. If attending the meeting is less important to you than washing your hair, it is time to get off that board.

Timing

Duration of the Meeting

Does the group have a fixed duration for the meeting? Some meetings, particularly meetings held virtually, have a time limit of one hour.

There is a trade-off on meeting duration. If you are having shorter meetings, you are probably having more frequent meetings. Virtual meetings are generally shorter. If a group has to travel to get together, people would generally like to have longer but less-frequent meetings. You don't want to take a plane to get to an hour-long meeting.

A full day meeting might be the norm for a group that only meets quarterly. If you want a one-hour meeting, is it going to be every week?

Notice

How much notice should be given when a participant cannot make the meeting? There should be a policy about this.

The minutes will show who attended, who sent their regrets, who was late, and who was absent. What gets measured, gets done – so measure this. If people see their name on the next meeting minutes as being late or absent, they might reconsider their decision about attending the next meeting.

Quorum

__Quorum is the minimum number of people who need to be present at a meeting so the decisions made will be legal.__

A typical quorum is half of the members plus one. In some groups, the chair will not have a vote, or sometimes the chair can only vote if the vote is tied. If the chair does not have a vote, quorum is calculated without considering the chair.

To Do

- ✓ Establish a meeting schedule, either at a regular time or set the meeting dates for the coming year. If you have to reschedule a meeting, use software to avoid wasting everyone's time.

- ✓ Establish a meeting duration.

- ✓ Develop a policy on what is considered quorum for your meetings.

- ✓ Make a policy about who is dealing with the scheduling administration, calling people, tracking quorum, and so forth.

- ✓ Make a policy about how many days notice is required if the participant cannot make the meeting.

6. Virtual Meetings

Virtual meetings have become more common since the pandemic started in 2020. There are advantages to virtual meetings and disadvantages. Most people have shortened their meetings when they hold them virtually.

Zoom fatigue occurs when people become tired of being on screen. Hiding the self view sometimes helps. It allows you to see the other people without watching yourself.

Agendas

Preparation of an agenda changes for a virtual meeting. Most meetings need to be shorter to hold the attention of the participants. You can generally count on there being less participation. Engagement is more difficult.

Frequency

If your virtual meetings are going to be shorter, then you need to have shorter agendas, less content for each meeting and thus more frequent meetings.

People used to have long meetings because some participants had to travel to attend the meeting. Now that the meeting is virtual and there is no travel, maybe shorter meetings are a better idea.

Polling

Instead of calling for a vote, the meeting host can set up a poll, in the video-conferencing software program (Zoom, Teams, GoToMeeting, WebEx, or whatever software you use) that asks the questions, and the participants can answer anonymously.

These polls will have to be set up by the meeting organizer, and the agenda should indicate that the vote will be held electronically.

Meeting Credentials or Signing In

The first part of the agenda might be the details or passwords that the participants need to join the meeting.

Security is a concern with virtual meetings. Most groups will establish a password to ensure that only authorized attendees will be able to get on the call. A waiting room is a best practice as well. This allows the host, who should be the chair, to control who is granted entry to the meeting.

Instructions should be given to the participants ahead of time so they are ready to go with the meeting software. If training is required, it should be done ahead of the actual meeting. Everyone has been in a meeting where a participant does not know how to unmute themselves and are talking away, and all you can see is their lips moving, like in a silent movie.

There is less and less need for training as more people attend virtual meetings, but if you do have a new person who needs training, you should find that out before everyone is on the call.

People can contribute to the meeting by bringing information to share, either by screen sharing or a link in the chat. Of course, materials should be provided before the meeting so the participants can review before the meeting.

To Do

- ✓ Establish your policies for holding virtual meetings: whether people will be asked to turn on their video or not, turn off their sound at the beginning of the meeting or not, whether participants in the meeting can share their screens or just the host, and so forth.

7 Confidential Items and Conflicts of Interest

Confidential Items

ARE THERE ANY items on the agenda that could be considered confidential? If so, how do you make sure that people who should not have access don't see the agenda?

The organization will have defined what information is confidential and developed policies to handle confidential matters. If there is any mention of confidential information on an agenda, then the agenda itself should be marked confidential. And all the rules that take place when there is a confidential item must be followed.

Circulation of Agenda

Is the agenda circulated electronically by email or text, or by mail or courier – or maybe a secure part of the website. The agenda must be marked confidential if there are confidential items on the agenda.

CIRCULATED ELECTRONICALLY

If the agenda is circulated electronically, controls are still needed. Will the agenda be encrypted? Will participants need a password to open the agenda?

If the participants are able to print out the agenda, they must be cautioned about maintaining confidentiality. If a board member prints out an encrypted, password-protected agenda, the printout must be safeguarded. They should not leave this paper anywhere where unauthorized people could see it.

Some groups have established secure email accounts for their meeting participants. They hope the recipient will not be sharing the email with family members.

CIRCULATED BY MAIL

If you mail the agenda out to participants, you must mark the envelope private and confidential. The recipient should be warned that assistants who open their mail must not open this confidential agenda.

Mark the front and the back of an envelope private and confidential in case someone is in the habit of opening all the mail and then sorting it out. Some people may open the mail without looking at the front of the envelope.

SECURE PART OF THE WEBSITE

The best practice is to have a secure part of the

organization's website where people can sign in to see items like the agenda and the minutes. A further safeguard would be to disable the print function on the webpage. In that way, you are very confident that the participant is not going to be printing out the documents and leaving them lying around unsecured.

You might still have people who show the screen to someone else, but there is no way to prevent that.

If you have participants who break the confidentiality of the agenda and tell other people what is on the agenda, ask them to leave the board or the committee.

Disposal of the Agenda

If there is confidential information on the agenda, this agenda must be disposed of in a confidential manner. If it is on paper, then the paper should be shredded or burned.

If the agenda was circulated via email, the recipient should be encouraged to delete the emails once the meetings have been held. Your organization should create a policy about email security, and of course participants should be made aware of the policies of the organization.

Train the Participants

Confidentiality should be a concern for every organization. If there is confidential material, it needs to be identified and protected from its creation through to its disposal.

The best way to protect the information is for everyone who handles it to be aware of the rules and procedures laid down by the privacy officer. We can have fancy electronic protocols, but they are all defeated when a participant tells their friends all about the confidential information being discussed at the meetings.

Rules do not work if they are not being followed.

Privacy Officer

The privacy officer or privacy department of an organization will provide guidelines on what can be included on an agenda. Ensure the agenda follows the guidelines set out by your organization.

Conflict of Interest

Usually, a particular attendee has a conflict of interest with only a part of the agenda. The agenda has to be customized so the conflicted member does not get the information that they should not see. This is a complicated task if there are multiple members with conflicts.

The meeting will also be complicated as the members who have a conflict must recuse themselves from the portion of the meeting in which the conflicted matter is being discussed. The agenda will list all the matters being discussed; it is the meeting preparation package that must be customized for each participant.

In Camera

What does in camera mean? It is Latin for "in the room." This is a secret part of the meeting. The purpose is usually to discuss a legal matter or an employee matter.

The way in camera is applied at a meeting can vary among groups. Management and guests are generally not permitted in camera, except for, perhaps, a lawyer who is assisting the board with a legal matter.

Used Sparingly

Moving a meeting in camera means there will be no public sharing of the discussion that takes place. Depending on the type of meeting, this can be a contentious decision. One of the principles of governance is transparency, and an in camera meeting is not transparent. If there is a lot of in camera meetings, the stakeholders are going to be restless. They will wonder what is going on.

Eventually, however the decisions made in the in camera meeting will be published. The in camera portion is for the discussion. Once conclusions are reached and the group exits the in camera part of the meeting, the members will make and pass the motion. If there are employment issues, the board could emerge from the in camera part of the meeting and announce that the pay raises have now been approved. The employees will never hear the discussion leading up to the decision.

If a board is deciding whether to sue someone, or if

they are being sued themselves, in camera meetings are necessary. You don't talk legal strategy at a meeting where the minutes are going to be circulated. In this case, the board could emerge from an in camera meeting to announce they are filing suit against someone.

Always on the Agenda

Another approach to in camera meetings is to have one scheduled as a routine part of the meeting, perhaps at the end of the regular meeting after the adjournment. The board thanks any guests for their attendance, they thank management, and they ask everyone other than the board to leave.

The board looks around the table at each other and asks, "Is there anything we need to discuss?" This meeting could be over quickly. The benefit of having the in camera always on the agenda is a reduction in drama. Staff and management get used to the idea. They are not worried about why the board is having an in camera meeting, because they always have an in camera meeting.

Typically, on the agenda, all that will be said is "in camera" and a time for when this will start and end, if it is your habit to record times on the agenda.

However, the participants who will be discussing an in camera item do need to know what it is about, so a separate communication will need to be made.

The participants invited to an in camera meeting will

need to be sent an agenda and information package. This will need to be handled in a confidential manner. No one except those invited to the in camera portion should ever be able to see the agenda or the minutes of this part of the meeting.

To Do

Confidentiality

- ✓ Determine whether the organization has any confidential matters that need to be put on the agenda.

- ✓ Establish a policy for how the minutes, agenda, and other materials are to be kept confidential.

- ✓ Organize training for the participants on how to deal with confidential matters, if needed.

Conflict of Interest

- ✓ Establish a conflict-of-interest policy and outline procedures for dealing with the situation.

In Camera

- ✓ Establish a policy on which topics should be handled by an in camera meeting. Usual examples include legal and employee matters.

8 Annual General Meetings

The AGM is an official meeting where very particular things must take place.

The most important part of this meeting is the election of the board of directors. This is the meeting where the membership or shareholders get to appoint the people who will make the decisions for them for the coming year.

In not-for-profit organizations, the members appoint the board of directors. If the organization is a business, the shareholders will vote in the board. In either case, this is the only time when the regular members get to make important decisions. After this, the decisions are in the hands of the directors until the next AGM.

The other main function of the AGM is the presentation of the annual financial statements for approval. If there is an auditor, this meeting is when the auditor will be appointed.

The typical AGM agenda goes like this:

1. Call to order
2. Approval of the agenda
3. Review and approval of last years AGM minutes
4. Reports
5. Approval of the annual financial statements
6. Appointment of the auditor (if applicable)
7. Call for nominations for the board
8. Election of the board
9. Announcement of the elected directors
10. Adjournment

Some groups have public speakers present at their meetings to improve attendance. Most people, with good reason, think that an AGM is a pretty dry event.

If you want more people to attend, you might need comedians or a wonderful meal.

Preparation for the Annual General Meeting

The preparation for an AGM can take some time. Developing a roster of qualified candidates for the election of directors can be a year-round activity for the nominating committee. A director can be elected to a multiple-year term. If they are elected for three years, then for the next two years their spot on the board is filled, and no election is needed for that spot.

A careful organization will make sure there are some seats coming up each year for election to avoid having all the board terms expire at one time. You do not want to have to replace an entire board at one AGM.

The agenda for the AGM will be circulated to the members of the organization ahead of time with the resumés of the potential board members included. The bylaws of the organization will determine how long before the meeting the AGM agenda must be circulated.

The participants in an AGM will be all the members — if the group is a not-for-profit organization, or all the shareholders — if the organization is a business. It is not expected that all members or shareholders will actually show up.

The election takes place with the people who show up. You need some percentage of all the members or shareholders to be in attendance for the meeting to have a quorum. That percentage will be determined by the bylaws.

If you have quorum, then the election will take place. A director will be elected if 50 percent of the people in attendance vote in favour of their election.

Supermajority

Some items on the agenda might require a supermajority, which is usually 75 percent of the members in favour of the motion. A special resolution, such as a bylaw change, requires a supermajority.

If a bylaw change is on the agenda, then attendance will be more important. You may need a good turnout to have a quorum to make the change.

To Do

- ✓ The nominating committee must make sure that there is a list of qualified candidates for the shareholders to choose from at the meeting.

- ✓ Develop a generic agenda on which to base each individual AGM. Include the minimum agenda items and add any items unique to the organization.

- ✓ Decide well ahead of time whether you want to have a great meal or a popular speaker at the event to get a good turnout.

- ✓ Circulate the AGM agenda at the prescribed time ahead of the meeting.

- ✓ Determine what quorum for the meeting is and whether any items need a supermajority.

9 Receiving an Agenda – A Guide for Participants

Scheduling

MAKE SURE ALL the meetings are on your calendar. It is your responsibility to attend every meeting.

Review the Agenda Promptly

Review the agenda as soon as possible and consider whether there are any items on the agenda where you might have a conflict of interest. If so, you need to follow the policy for your group about disclosing the conflict and recusing yourself from the relevant parts of the meeting. It is your responsibility to understand the conflict-of-interest policies set by your group.

Think about the Decisions

What do you think about the decisions that are going to be made at the next meeting? Do you understand the options? Is there any more information you would like to have before you decide? Contact the chair and explain what you would like to know. It is possible the information can be forwarded to you. Or, the chair can get the information before the meeting. Chances are that if you are looking for something then others in the group will be as well.

Open Your Mind

Are you ready to listen to the other people in the meeting who may have different opinions? You can come to the meeting with your decisions in your mind, but you should be prepared to change your mind if other participants bring up something you had not thought about. You should be open to changing your mind. If you hear a good argument at the meeting, will you change how you vote on a motion? I hope so. Being willing to listen to other people and consider whether they have a good point will help the group make the best decisions.

These days there is divisiveness in certain groups. Members of one group will disagree with another group because that is a part of their identity. I have heard politicians express the sentiment that disagreeing with the other party is their job. You don't need this at your meetings.

Years ago, I spent time with a board that had two members who did not get along. I will call them Jill and Jack. If Jack was in favour of a motion, Jill was opposed, and she did not need to know what the motion was about, and vice versa. They could not even agree on a motion to adjourn. This is not appropriate meeting participant behaviour. This board was dysfunctional!

The appropriate strategy is to remove both people because neither of them have an open mind, and that is necessary to do a good job as a board member.

Behave Yourself

Part of the job of being a board member is to represent the interests of the organization, even when they conflict with your own interests. This is a part of representing others and satisfying your duty of care.

Plan to follow the rules at the meeting. Make sure you allow enough time to arrive at the meeting on time. Participants who arrive late are a disruption to the meeting.

Issues Not Personalities

The board will be discussing the issues not the personalities of the board member. You might think one of your board members is a fool, but you are not allowed to say so. You might still agree with this person, even though they are a fool and you are a genius.

When you disagree with someone, you are disagreeing

with their opinion, not them personally. People need to be able to talk about differences of opinion without getting their feelings hurt or feeling disrespected.

To Do

✓ Your organization might consider having a guide for new members, explaining their responsibilities. Ask your chair for this.

Glossary

Adjourn – the end of a meeting. Someone makes a motion to adjourn and, at that time, the meeting is over.

Agenda – a plan for the meeting. The agenda could be a standard listing of all the items to be discussed at a board meeting, which will be the same each time. An agenda could be a list of the decisions to be made.

Annotate – an ability for a participant to "write" on the host's screen during a virtual meeting. This ability can be turned on or off by the host.

Annual general meeting – the meeting of members to elect the board, approve the annual financial statements and appoint an auditor.

Board – a short form of "board of directors," "board of governors," and so forth. A board is elected by the members at the annual general meeting to oversee the running of the organization.

Board package – the information circulated to participants prior to any meeting. The expectation is that it will be read prior to the meeting taking place.

Call to order – the beginning of a meeting, where the chair lets the participant know that the meeting is about to begin. The minutes start being taken at this point.

Chair or chairperson – the person at the meeting who leads the discussion and is responsible for keeping the meeting on schedule and compliant with the rules.

Chat – the ability to type comments into a section of the screen during a virtual meeting. This ability can be turned on or off by the host.

Committee – a group with a specific task who meets and reports to the board. Typical examples are the audit committee, finance committee, and human resource committee.

Guest – a person who is invited to a meeting. They do not have a vote but are allowed to make comments. A guest can be at a meeting for a specific period of time to discuss some issue. For example, a lawyer might come to a meeting to talk about potential litigation.

Majority – the percentage of the participants who must vote in favour of a motion for it to be approved. This figure is usually more than 50 percent of the participants.

Meeting – a group of people (more than one person) gathering to make decisions. The meeting can be as formal as the board meeting of a corporation or as casual as two people deciding about lunch.

Meeting package – (usually called board package) the information circulated to participants prior to any meeting. The expectation is that it will be read prior to the meeting taking place.

Member – a person who has privileges because of joining an organization.

Minutes – the record of what was accomplished at the meeting. This can be a written record or audio and video recordings.

Motion – a series of conversations at a meeting that result in a decision being voted on by the group. For example, John says, "I move to approve the agenda." The chair says, "Do I have a seconder?" Sally says, "I second that motion." The chair says, "All those in favour signify by saying "aye." Everyone says aye, and the motion is passed, which means that the agenda has been approved. A motion may also be called a resolution.

Participant – a person attending a meeting who can vote.

Quorum – the minimum number of participants required to be in attendance at a meeting before the meeting can make any official decisions.

Recusal – a person leaves a meeting for a period of time and then returns. For example, when a participant has a conflict of interest with an item being discussed and leaves the meeting when the item is being discussed.

Rules of order – a set of rules used to run a meeting. For example, *Bourinot's Rules of Order* or *Robert's Rules of Order* contain instructions on how to make a motion, get the chairs attention, and be respectful.

Supermajority – the percentage of the participants who must approve a special resolution, such as a bylaw change. A supermajority is typically 75 percent or at least 67 percent.

Appendix A
Policies to Consider

WRITTEN POLICIES ARE the best practice. The organization should take the time to discuss and document the values they want exhibited at the organization's meetings.

Here are some examples of policies that you can choose from. They are just examples . . . Feel free to make your own if these don't fit your organization.

Meeting Administration

Who can add items to the agenda?

Determining who is allowed to add items to the agenda will vary with the type of meetings. In general, only members of the group will be allowed to add items to the agenda for that group.

1. Items may be added to the agenda by any member of the committee or by the board who supervises the committee. When the board sends an agenda item to committee this is done by motion.

2. Items may be added to the agenda by any

committee member and any board member. The agenda requires a majority to agree before it is approved.

3. Items may be added to the agenda by any committee member or the executive team as a whole.

When can items be added to the agenda?

Each group will decide when items may be added to an agenda: before a meeting, at the start of a meeting, or throughout the meeting.

1. The agenda is circulated prior to the meeting, and items can be added by any member of the board up to the time when the agenda is finalized. No items may be added to the agenda at the time of the meeting unless the item is an emergency. An emergency is defined as an item that is both urgent and time sensitive. The participants will vote on whether an item can be considered an emergency and therefore added to the agenda at the last minute.

2. For an item to be added to the agenda at the time of the meeting, the item must be both urgent and crucial – the item needs to be decided immediately or there will be grave damage done to the organization.

3. Anyone can add items to the agenda at the start of each meeting.

4. Anyone can add items to the agenda throughout the meeting.

How many days before the meeting is the agenda circulated?

Circulating an agenda before the meeting allows participants time to prepare for the meeting and allows the group to carefully consider what matters should be discussed at the meeting.

1. The agenda must be circulated no later than seven days before the meeting. Additions to the agenda must be submitted five days before the meeting. The agenda is approved and closed three days before the meeting.

2. The agenda must be circulated no later than three days before the meeting. Additions to the agenda must be submitted two days before the meeting. The agenda is approved and closed the day before the meeting.

3. The agenda is circulated at the meeting. Additions to the agenda are made at that time.

Is there a standard agenda format?

Groups may find that a standard agenda format allows them to prepare for a meeting more quickly. The decisions about the order of items on an agenda impact on the flow of the meeting. These decisions can be made when initially preparing the standard agenda and then used until a change is needed.

1. A standard format is used for every meeting. Changes to the standard format can only be made if approved by the governance committee.

2. We do not use a standard agenda format. The format is determined by the chairperson each meeting.

3. We have a standard agenda format that is revised each year.

4. We have a standard agenda format that is revised as needed.

Do you have a strategic planning section on every agenda?

If the group has a strategic plan, they should tie this strategic plan into their board meetings. Clearly if the time has been spent to create the strategic plan, then the plan should be used to direct and manage activities of the group.

1. The progress in implementing our strategic plan is reported each board meeting. This is a standard agenda item.

2. Our strategic plan includes a listing of what will be accomplished during each time period on the plan, and the agenda for meetings includes this information.

3. For each item on the agenda, we indicate how it is tied into the strategic plan.
4. We don't have a strategic plan.

Who may miss a meeting?

Members of a group are expected to attend the meetings of that group. Acceptable reasons for missing a meeting must be established.

1. All members are expected to attend all the meetings. More than two absences in a year will result in the board member being asked to leave the organization.

2. All members are expected to attend all the meetings. More than three absences in a year will result in the board member being asked to leave the organization.

3. All members are expected to attend all meetings. Decisions will be made on a case-by-case basis concerning whether a member has missed too many meetings.

4. Missing a meeting due to attending an event on behalf of the organization will not be recorded as an absence for the purposes of the attendance policy.

5. Participants who are absent because they are attending to board business elsewhere will not be considered absent. This permission should be

obtained before the meeting, preferably at the time the agenda is circulated.

How to send regrets?

Regrets are sent when a board member knows they are going to miss a meeting. Usually, the earlier regrets can be sent the better to allow for decisions about cancelling and rescheduling meetings.

1. A member is expected to send regrets as soon as they are aware they will be missing a meeting.
2. Regrets must be sent in as soon as the agenda is received.
3. Regrets must be sent in no later than five days before any meeting.
4. Inclement weather will be taken into consideration when recording whether missing a meeting is an allowable absence.
5. Regrets will be received at any time up to the start of the meeting.

How often should policy review be added to the agenda?

Policy review is an important part of board governance.

1. One or more policies should be reviewed at every meeting to ensure that all policies are reviewed on a three-year cycle.
2. Policies should be reviewed when anyone on the

board feels a policy is out of date or that a new policy should be developed.

3. One third of all policies should be reviewed each year, and a separate meeting should be called to perform this review.

Meeting Planning Policies

Who may attend the meeting?

For each meeting held by a group, who is allowed to attend and who might be invited as a guest should be determined.

1. Only board members and those who are invited by the board may attend board meetings. The executive director is typically invited to the board meeting.
2. Our meetings are open to anyone who wishes to attend, even non-members.
3. Our meetings are open to any member who wishes to attend.
4. Our meetings are only open to board members and staff. If others wish to attend, this permission may be granted, but must be requested three days before the meeting.

How long are the meetings?

The length of a meeting should be determined as a part of the agenda process. Groups will make the trade-off between less frequent but longer meetings and more frequent but shorter meetings. Board and committee meetings may have different policies.

1. Board meetings may be no longer than three hours.
2. Board meetings held in person may be no longer than four hours, board meetings held virtually may be no longer than ninety minutes.
3. Board meetings do not have a fixed length.
4. Committee meetings may be no longer than one and a half hours.
5. Committee meetings held in person may be no longer than two hours; committee meetings held virtually may be no longer than ninety minutes.
6. Committee meetings do not have a fixed length.

When are board meetings held?

Setting a standard meeting time will improve attendance as will planning the meetings a year at a time.

1. Board meetings are held on the first Wednesday evening of each month, except for the month of August during which there will be no meetings.

2. Board meetings are scheduled at the last meeting of the year, for the coming year.
3. Board meetings are called when necessary.
4. The next board meeting is scheduled at the end of each current meeting.

When and how is conflict of interest declared?

Conflict of interest is a serious matter. Group members need to know when and how to declare their conflicts of interest.

1. A board member must declare any conflict of interest in writing to the governance committee as soon as they become aware of the conflict.
2. When a board member receives a proposed agenda, they should review this agenda and determine immediately whether they are in conflict with any of the items and advise the chair.
3. All board members will sign an annual declaration disclosing all conflicts of interest and will update this declaration during the year as new conflicts arise.

How will the meeting preparation packages be distributed?

For members to prepare for a meeting, they must have access to the meeting materials.

1. The information needed to prepare for a meeting

will be emailed to the members a minimum of six days before the meeting. If there is any confidential information in this package, the recipient will safeguard the package in an appropriate manner.

2. The information needed to prepare for a meeting will be made available on the members-only portion of the organization's website one week before every meeting.

3. Any material that is distributed to the members prior to a meeting will be maintained in a separate password-protected file and will be available to the participants for the same time period as the minutes.

How will participants maintain confidentiality?

Board members and employees are prohibited from sharing any confidential information in their possession with any person who is not authorized to know this information.

1. Board members and employees are required to maintain confidentiality. This includes keeping written material in a secure location, safeguarding passwords for digital information, and not telling anyone who is not authorized to hear the information. This policy applies before and after any board meeting and continues after the participant leaves the organization.

2. Board members and employees are required to

maintain confidentiality. This is done through whatever means necessary by safeguarding confidential material no matter what form it takes. This policy always applies, even after participants leave the organization.

3. Board members and employees are expected to maintain confidentiality of all information even after leaving the organization.

How many members must be present to constitute a meeting?

The number of participants needed in attendance for the meeting to be considered valid for business to be conducted needs to be established. This may have been done in the bylaws.

1. Quorum is half the board plus one. Our twelve-member board has a quorum of seven attendees.

2. Quorum is 50 percent or more of the board members. Our twelve-member board has a quorum of six.

3. Quorum is five members in attendance.

What are the requirements of the participants?

The group may have an entire handbook on what is expected of members. This policy is only related to meeting attendance.

1. Participants are expected to come to the meetings

prepared to discuss the items on the agenda. Material circulated prior to the meeting should be read before the meeting commences. Participants should request any additional information needed before the meeting commences.

2. Participants are expected to review the minutes as soon as convenient after they receive the minutes. Minutes are not to be reviewed at the time of the subsequent meeting. Any differences in the minutes based on this review must be communicated to the minute taker prior to the meeting.

3. Participants are expected to come to the meetings with an open mind, ready to listen to the other attendees and change their minds as necessary about an issue.

4. Participants are expected to behave in a respectful manner toward the chair and other participants and to adhere to the rules of the meeting.

During-the-Meeting Policies

When do we hold in camera meetings?

1. We have in camera meetings to discuss legal matters and employment issues. All other decisions are made at regular meetings.

How do we enforce respectful behaviour?

1. The person who is speaking at the meeting may not be interrupted by any one other than the chairperson. The chairperson will stop all interruptions. Participants who continue to interrupt after being warned by the chair will be asked to leave the meeting, and participants who are asked to leave more than one meeting will be asked to leave the board.

2. All members will behave in a respectful manner toward all the other participants. At no time will name calling or demeaning another person be allowed. Our meetings are a safe space for people to express their views; the only exception is that we do not tolerate hate speech.

How do we make a motion?

1. When a participant wants to make a motion, or to speak, they should raise their hand until the chair nods at them. The chair will keep a list of who wishes to speak next so that participants are able to speak in turn.

2. The topic is introduced, the members have a discussion, and then the motion is made. The motion will be seconded and then the vote taken. There is no discussion after the motion has been made.

3. The motion is made and seconded, the members have a discussion, and then the vote is taken.

How do we vote?

Voting can happen in a variety of ways at meetings. The smaller the meeting, the less formal the voting procedure.

1. Votes will be taken verbally unless the results of the vote are not clear, in which case the vote can be done by a show of hands. In rare cases where the items being voted on are contentious, the vote can be taken by secret ballot. Any participant can ask for the vote to be taken by secret ballot. The chair can also make this determination.
2. Votes are always done by secret ballot.
3. Votes are done by a show of hands.

Groups will establish the percentage of participants voting in favour of a motion for it to pass. This is called a majority.

1. A majority for the purposes of passing a motion is any percentage of participants greater than 50 percent.
2. A majority is one person more than 50 percent. If there are eight people at a meeting, then more than four of them must vote in favour for the motion to pass.

A super majority is required to pass any bylaw changes.

1. Our super majority amount is 75 percent.

2. Our super majority amount is two thirds (66.67 percent).
3. Our super majority amount is 90 percent.

How do we evaluate meetings?

Determining whether a meeting was effective is required if meetings are going to be effective in the future. Improvement is always desirable.

1. The second-last item on the agenda will be the evaluation of the meeting to determine whether the goals were achieved and the meeting was carried out in an effective and respectful manner.
2. Meetings will be evaluated by sending a questionnaire out to each participant after the meeting is over.
3. One meeting a year is devoted to discussing how our meetings are being conducted.

Virtual Meeting Policies

The policies for an in-person meeting will still apply. In addition, there are some policies specific to virtual meetings.

How do we get into the meeting and what happens if we are late?

Virtual meetings are generally restricted to those participants who have been sent an invite.

1. All virtual meetings must have a password or other method of restricting access to only those who were invited. Participants will be reminded that no others should be listening to the meeting.
2. The waiting room will be enabled and no participant who arrives more than ten minutes late will be admitted.
3. All members are expected to arrive on time for all meetings. The meeting will start on time. Any member who arrives more than ten minutes late will not be allowed to attend the meeting and will be noted as being absent from the meeting.

What are the communication rules during the meeting?

1. Audio must be muted unless the person is speaking, and the video must be on during the meeting.
2. There will be a breakout room set up so that participants who have a conflict of interest can leave the main meeting.
3. Participants will be able to use the chat function and to annotate any shared screen.

Appendix A: Policies to Consider

MAKING A MOTION

1. When a participant wants to make a motion, or to speak, they should use the raise-hand function until the chair nods at them. The chair will keep a list of who wishes to speak next so that participants are able to speak in turn.
2. Participants may speak without asking.

EVALUATION

1. The host of the meeting – who in most cases should be the chair – sets up the polls for meeting evaluation.
2. There is no evaluation of the meeting.

VOTING

1. Participants vote on motions using the chat feature, and the minute taker performs the count.
2. Participants vote on motions using the polling function, which is set up ahead of the meeting.
3. Participants vote on motions by unmuting themselves and saying either aye or nay.
4. Participants vote on motions by physically raising their hands (if all participants have video on) in such a way that the chair can see them and count them.

Annual General Meeting Policies

Many of the policies for the annual general meeting (AGM) will be established in the bylaws. In addition, all the usual meeting policies apply. An AGM differs from a regular meeting in the amount of notice given and the attendance.

1. The board advertises the AGM on social and traditional media for thirty days before the meeting takes place.

2. The board emails a call to meeting notice with all the documentation attached to all the members.

3. Anyone may attend our AGM; it is open to the public.

Appendix B
Consolidated List of Things to Do

Do you need a meeting?

- ✓ Analyze whether each meeting is necessary or if there might be another way to achieve the goal. See if you can eliminate 10 percent of the meetings on your schedule and replace them with shared documents or an email thread.

- ✓ Determine what the goal is for each of these meetings you deem necessary.

How do you create the agenda?

- ✓ Develop a generic agenda on which to base each individual meeting's agenda. Include the minimum agenda items and add any items unique to the organization.

- ✓ Decide whether to use a consent agenda for those reports that don't need discussion.

- ✓ Decide whether you will have any actions from the strategic plan (if you have one) on your agenda.

- ✓ Decide how your organization deals with policy review: Do you need to schedule an annual or quarterly policy review meeting? Or is there a committee? Or maybe you should put the policy review on each meeting agenda?

- ✓ For every standard meeting, set a policy about the development of the agenda and document the process. Document who is allowed to add items to the agenda, how the agenda is circulated, how it is approved, how differences of opinion concerning the agenda will be dealt with, and so forth.

- ✓ The duration for the meeting should also be established, and you may want to assign a time to each agenda item.

- ✓ Create a set of meeting evaluation questions for distribution at the end of the meeting.

Who comes to the meetings?

- ✓ Decide who is and is not invited to the meeting: ex-officio members, SMEs, committee chairs, observers. Set a time limit for re-evaluating when some office is needed on the board and when they are not.

- ✓ Determine whether you have a way to change who is invited or to uninvite someone who has been attending the meeting, either for their behaviour or because they are not contributing.

- ✓ Your organization might consider having a guide for new members, explaining their responsibilities.

What do you do with the draft agenda?

- ✓ Establish a policy about circulating the agenda. This policy should include how it is circulated, who gets it, how long before the meeting is it circulated, and the methods and deadlines to be used to add items to the agenda or to ask for items to be removed.

How do you schedule the meeting?

- ✓ Establish a meeting schedule, either at a regular time or set the meeting dates for the coming year. If you have to reschedule a meeting, use software to avoid wasting everyone's time.

- ✓ Establish a meeting duration.

- ✓ Develop a policy on what is considered quorum for your meetings.

- ✓ Make a policy about who is dealing with the scheduling administration, calling people, tracking quorum, and so forth.

- ✓ Make a policy about how many days notice is required if the participant cannot make the meeting.

How do you hold a virtual meeting?

✓ Establish your policies for holding virtual meetings: whether people will be asked to turn on their video or not, turn off their sound at the beginning of the meeting or not, whether participants in the meeting can share their screens or just the host, and so forth.

How do you deal with confidential items and conflicts of interest?

CONFIDENTIALITY

✓ Determine whether the organization has any confidential matters that need to be put on the agenda.

✓ Establish a policy for how the minutes, agenda, and other materials are to be kept confidential.

✓ Organize training for the participants on how to deal with confidential matters, if needed.

CONFLICT OF INTEREST

✓ Establish a conflict-of-interest policy and outline procedures for dealing with the situation.

IN CAMERA

✓ Establish a policy on which topics should be handled by an in camera meeting. Usual examples include legal and employee matters.

How do you prepare for the AGM?

- ✓ The nominating committee must make sure that there is a list of qualified candidates for the shareholders to choose from at the meeting.

- ✓ Develop a generic agenda on which to base each individual AGM. Include the minimum agenda items and add any items unique to the organization.

Other Books by Debi J. Peverill

Basic Board Governance

Budgeting Essentials

Can Your Business be Sold?

Every Canadian's Guide to Financial Prosperity

Painless Financial Literacy

Starting a Successful Business

Ten Tax Traps to Avoid

About the Author

DEBI J. PEVERILL has attended thousands of meetings during her decades-long career as a Chartered Accountant and a professional speaker.

Debi is a rare individual: an accountant with a sense of humour and no fear of public speaking. She has a particular interest in governance, taxation, and financial management.

Debi teaches courses in the Sobeys School of Business at Saint Mary's University, Halifax, runs her public accounting practice, and finds time to record helpful tips on LinkedIn, Twitter, and YouTube twice a week. She also writes on Medium and her own blog at DebiPeverill.ca.

She is the mother of two grown children and lives with her long-suffering husband in Lower Sackville, Nova Scotia.

For More Information

Twitter: @DebiPev

LinkedIn.com/in/DebiPeverill

YouTube.com/c/DebiPeverillPFTG

DebiPev.Medium.com

Peverill.ca (accounting business)
DebiPeverill.ca (financial tips)
PainlessFinancialTrainingGroup.ca (books and courses)

www.ingramcontent.com/pod-product-compliance
Lightning Source LLC
Chambersburg PA
CBHW050326230526
45471CB00005B/2368